Stop Calling Humans Black and White

Dr. R. Peprah-Gyamfi

Perseverance Books Ltd

Published by **Perseverance Books**

www.peprah-gyamfi.com
email: **info@peprah-gyamfi.com**

ISBN: 9781913285050
eISBN: 9781913285067

"So God created humankind in his image,
in the image of God he created them;
male and female he created them."

Genesis 1:27 (NRSV)

Acknowledgement

I am deeply grateful to aeon.co for the permission to republish the article 'How "white people" were invented by a playwright in 1613' by Ed Simons, originally published at https://aeon.co under Creative Commons.

Table of contents

Preamble

In Memory of George Floyd

2 6 May 2020: the UK was in total coronavirus lockdown. As a doctor, I am considered a key worker, so I was permitted to leave home for work. I was booked by my agency to work at a town about 90 minutes' drive from home.

The journey went through the English countryside; only a small portion of the journey was along a dual carriageway – the remainder was along a single-lane road with traffic travelling in each direction.

The journey along that stretch of single-lane road usually demands a lot of patience on the part of the driver. A few factors account for that. There is a lot of farmland along the way. One's smooth ride is frequently interrupted by slow-moving lorries and tractors.

The road also passes through several small settlements; speed restrictions are in place in several areas.

On a normal working day, it usually takes me around 90 minutes to travel the distance of about 70 miles.

As I set out from home on this occasion, I reckoned with the same duration for my journey.

Ach! I had forgotten I was living in a new era – the era of the coronavirus!

As already mentioned, UK was in lockdown. Apart from key workers like myself, hardly any travel was permitted.

So, the road was virtually deserted, giving me a free ride.

It was a lovely bright day in spring. The sun was shining; the sky was clear and blue. The vegetation on each side of the road was green, pure green. Nature appeared to be at peace with itself.

The day's session was particularly long – from 9am to 9pm – with a few breaks in between. The first break was from 12 noon to 1pm. As was my practice. I went online to check the news, so as to update myself with the happenings from around the world.

On clicking on BBC online news, I was confronted with an image of a police officer kneeling on the neck of an individual lying prostrate on a street, near a police vehicle. Accompanying the image was the news story headed: "Four Minnesota police officers fired after death of unarmed black man."

I was so horrified on viewing the accompanying video that for a while I thought I was not seeing right!

I knew the matter was already in the public domain. Still I decided to post it to my Facebook page, just in case someone had missed it. I thought of the comments to accompany it. In the end I ended up with the following:

"This has nothing to do with race – I believe in only the ONE and ONLY human race anyway. This has all to do with a human being behaving like an animal, period. I have nothing more to add to the matter!" (26/05/2020)

I did indeed reckon with public anger to the killing. Owing to the coronavirus pandemic and the restrictions on public gatherings, I reckoned initially with a limited public response in the form of demonstrations. Well, as it turned out, I was wrong.

Two days after my initial Facebook posting, I posted a scene showing an angry confrontation of demonstrators with police and commented as follows:

"Pitiful mankind! We are facing the threat of annihilation from naughty and cruel coronavirus! Instead of mobilizing our energies against the common foe, we are now at war with ourselves!! Almighty Father, please have mercy on pitiful and pathetic humankind!!!" (28/05/2020)

For the next several days, the matter would not let me rest, in particular as further details of the shocking incident emerged. In the course of the week, I saw a YouTube video of the teenage girl whose cell phone live recording of the events brought the matter into the public domain. In it she said something that could have also come from me– "I am traumatised". Indeed, for a long time after viewing the horrific scene recorded by her cell phone, I also felt traumatised.

I was traumatised not because the victim shared the same skin colour as myself. No, I was traumatised by the fact that another human being could go to the extent of kneeling on the neck of a fellow human being for a period exceeding eight minutes. The thought that, according to the reports, he kept pressing on the neck of the dying man, even as he was told the pulse of the victim could no longer be felt, compounded my distress.

For a while I felt ashamed to count myself among humanity. As a human being, I was ashamed that anyone could behave in that manner to a fellow human. I thought our common humanity taught us that when one sees a fellow human in an emergency, one either provides first aid or, if one is not in a position to do so, one calls for help.

I also considered the matter from the point of view of a medical doctor. I found it inconceivable that anyone, especially a police officer, would ever conceive the idea of applying sustained pressure on the neck, an area of the body containing important nerves and vessels leading to and from the brain, as well as important structures such as the gullet and the wind pipe. As one leading US law maker put it in her contribution to the debate that followed the appalling incident, it amounts to lynching. That, in my opinion, is what it really boils down to!

Over the next few days the events leading to the death of Mr George Floyd would not leave me in peace. As the comments that accompanied my first Facebook post on the matter revealed, my initial reaction was that the matter had nothing to do with race. As the days passed and I followed the public debate and discussions on the matter, it dawned on me that I was partially right in my assessment. In the sense that the term "race" is considered from the biogenetic aspect I was right in my conclusion that it had nothing to do with race, for biologists are of the opinion that there is indeed only one human race.

It is an open secret that the term "race" has in the meantime received another connotation that has, for example, led to the classification of people of African descent as belonging to a "black" race and Europeans on their part to a "white" race. Though such classifications are null and void from the point of view of organisms like Ebola, HIV and coronavirus, which attacks humans irrespective of their "race", some members of the human community accord huge importance to that classification, which in reality is imaginary, an artificial construct.

The question that then sprung in my mind as I continued to ponder the matter was– would the police officer in question have treated a person who looked exactly like himself, someone of his "race", in a similar manner?

Had that fellow learnt from childhood that since the colour black is associated with evil, humans designated black are inferior and not worthy of life?

Has that notion become so deeply engrained in his psyche/mind that even as he pressed on the neck of the dying man, he did not feel any sense of compassion for him, thinking he was so inferior, by virtue of his black colour, that death would not make any difference? I may be wrong in my assertion, but the fact that he kept both of his hands in his pocket, displayed a careless, unconcerned demeanour and kept pressing on George

Floyd's neck, even as his victim was suffocating to death and pleading for his life, left that impression on me.

That led me to reflect on the issue of the "racial" conflict that has been fanned by a section of people of European descent on the one hand and those people of African descent on the other hand over the years.

Why are there not that much "racial" tension between Europeans and Chinese or Europeans and Japanese? Why has this conflict between "blacks" and "whites" persisted for so long –simmering since the early fifteenth century, when Europeans first arrived on the African continent? I kept wondering.

The Europeans indeed also colonised the Americas, the Indian subcontinent, the Far East and several other parts of the world. Why then has the conflict between people of African descent vis a vis people of European descent persisted longer than others – and continues to persist even to this day. Why, why, why? I kept asking myself.

As I sought for the answers, even without consulting any textbooks three contributory factors came into my mind – the slave trade; the colonization of Africa by various European powers; and, lastly, the system initiated by the English, whereby people of European descent were classified as "whites" and those of African descent as "black".

The slave trade has ended; the colonisation of Africa has finished – but not so the classification of Africans as "black" and Europeans as "white".

Could ending the practise of designating Africans as "black", a colour associated with evil and all that is bad, lessen the negative perception the rest of the world has vis a vis people endowed with that type of skin colour?

Over the next few days, the events surrounding the brutal killing of the unarmed 46-year-old man and the issue of the negative perceptions accorded people of the "black" race occupied my mind.

That is not to say that, prior to the tragic death of Mr Floyd, the issue of the burden of being designated "black" had not occupied my thoughts.

Indeed, ever since I was big enough to reason, I have had difficulty coming to terms with the use of the term "black" to describe me. For God's sake, the colour of my skin is far from being black. Chocolate brown it could be called, but with all certainty not black. If that is not the case, who then had the audacity to describe me in a manner in which I was not created by my Maker! Indeed, even long before the George Floyd case hit the headlines, I had been seeking ways of seeking legal redress on the matter – a legal injunction calling for an end to the practise that, in my view, amounts to crass discrimination against me, a blatant infringement of my human rights, a situation that, in the past, has caused, and even as I write continues to cause, tremendous emotional distress and damage to my mental health.

The fact that I have kept quiet on the matter due to financial constraints does not imply I have completely given up on the matter.

Although, I do not presently have the financial means to pursue my case right up to the highest available international human rights court, the horrific scenes that unfolded on the streets of Minneapolis on 25 May 2020, caught on camera by the brave 17-year-old girl, has prompted me into action. How indeed can anyone remain on the sidelines in view of the horrible scenes caught on the cell phone video recording?

I have therefore decided to pursue an alternative course of action – a Plan B as it were.

So, as I await the opportunity to take legal action to pray that international legal experts redress the human right abuse against my person, I have decided in the meantime to bring my case before the peoples of the global village, the world jury, as it were.

So what is the core of my matter?

It is the following: I am calling for an end to the practice of calling humans "black" and "white".

In the next sections, I will present my case to the jury. I am not going to make only a verbal presentation; I will also provide evidence to substantiate my case.

Part one

A call for change

1

Stop calling humans black and white

L adies and gentlemen of the world jury, I bow before you in deep humility and honour.

Before I proceed to outline my case, I want to stress that this campaign was initiated not out of anger, scorn, resentment, or in the spirit of retaliation etc., but rather on a point of principle.

In his book *John North Willys*, Elbert Hubbard, the nineteenth-century American writer, publisher, artist, and philosopher, wrote: "Do nothing, say nothing, and be nothing, and you'll never be criticized." Well, for the sake of principle, I cannot "Do nothing, say nothing, and be nothing" concerning this fundamental issue of unfair, discriminatory, biased, non-objective classification of God's children into "black" for malice and "white" for innocence!

So, ladies and gentlemen of the jury, I herewith present my case. May I please beg you to pay close attention to the matter.

Presently, it is an accepted practice to call people of African descent "black" and those of European "white".

I would have had no difficulty with the matter if indeed the classification was objectively grounded –if indeed there were typically black and typically white individuals walking the surface of the earth.

That, however, is not the case. In other words, the classification is an artificial construct that is not at par with reality.

Since black is associated with evil and white good, designating humans in such a manner leads to negative stereotyping and stigmatisation.

Before I proceed any further, I want to take the jury to the very beginning of human existence – to the fundamental question of how humans came to populate the earth.

It is superfluous to mention here that there were no humans around to witness the very moment when the universe came into being. So the issue of how the universe came into being and how life on earth and, for that matter, human life began has been and continues to be a contentious issue. It is beyond the remit of the present discourse to reignite the huge debate that has been going on over centuries on the matter.

For the present discussion, I want to state that there are basically two main schools of thought on the matter.

On the one hand are those who believe that Almighty God created the universe and that it contains plants, birds of the air and land, fishes of the rivers and oceans, beasts of the land etc. As a climax of His creation, God created humans.

The second school of thought comprises those who either do not believe in God or, even if they do believe in God, hold the view that life developed gradually over millions of years by way of evolution. Concerning humans, this group holds the view that they evolved from ape-like beings. This book is not a forum for debate on the matter.

What then led to the various skin colours of humans?

First, I will look at the matter from the God the Creator version. Whilst trying to maintain neutrality on the issue at hand, I want to make it known to the jury that I personally ascribe to the Creator God version of how the universe and human life came into existence in the universe. The creation story in Genesis on which this group base their case does not explicitly deal with the matter of how the various skin colouration came into being. Based on my own insight in the matter, an insight acquired by way of my professional background, I dare to present this explanation. I want to stress that this is my own subjective view on the matter – the jury may choose to dismiss or accept it.

As already mentioned, I believe that Almighty God created humans. Based on the Bible the original parents of humankind were Adam and Eve.

To be protected from the harmful effects of the ultra-violet (UV) rays of the sun, the absorption of which can lead to skin cancer, the Creator God endowed the epidermis, the outer layer of the human skin with cells known as melanocytes. It is worth noting that melanocytes are distributed equally in skins of all humans, irrespective of which population group they belong to.

The function of melanocytes is the production of melanin. Melanin on its part shields the body from the harmful effect of UV radiation.

As humans began to multiply on earth, they migrated to various parts of the globe. Humans who migrated to areas of abundant sunshine needed considerable amounts of melanin to shield them against the harmful effects of the ever-present sunshine. To adapt to the new environment, over the years, the cells responsible for the production of the protective melanin became permanently active in performing their vital function of melanin production. The abundance of melanin endowed the population a skin hue from light brown to the darkest brown.

Conversely, the melanocytes of fellow humans who settled in the cold climatic zone where the sun barely shone did not need as much protection from the sun – certainly not to the same extent as did those who settled in the sun. Over the years, the cells responsible for the production of the pigment became somewhat dormant, leaving them with a pale hue of skin.

Many people do not believe in a Creator God as the originator of life on earth. Concerning the differing skin colours of humans, they hold the view that the difference developed through the principle of natural selection and adaptation. They hold to the view that the skins of humans who after the evolutionary process found themselves in the sunny areas of the planet adapted themselves to the exposure through the production of melanin in quantities needed to protect their skins from the harmful effect of UV radiation – hence the typically dark-skinned colour of people of African descent.

Certainly these are very simplified versions of the two prevailing but opposing viewpoints on the issue of the beginning of mankind. This is not the forum for a detailed discussion on the matter.

Whether one believes in a Creator God or in evolution, one fact remains crystal clear – there are no purely white and purely black humans on earth. There are indeed those whose skin colour could be described as darkest brown, approaching black, but pure black – the way I can without doubt refer to the colour of the laptop I am writing on – there are none. The converse is true – there are fellow humans who have a really light complexion, which could be regarded as approaching white, but a really white skin-coloured person, whose complexion could be described as "as white as snow", I am yet to meet.

So when did it all begin? When did humans begin to call a section of the human population black and another section white? How did we end up with the concept of the "black" and "white" human race?

Before I tackle that issue, I want to take the jury to the era of European exploration. Prior to the period of European expeditions to other lands, the idea of "white" and "black" was non-existent. It is beyond the remit of this discourse to delve deep into the complex theme of European exploration, conquest and subsequent exploitation of other population groups. I only want to provide a brief overview.

Towards the end of the fifteenth century, European explorers arrived on the west African coast. Human beings, who by virtue of their stay in the cold climates had over the years developed a fair skin complexion, for the first time came into contact with fellow humans who had developed various shades of dark skin complexions due to their exposure to the sun. I can imagine how surprised both parties were at the very first meeting – humans who, but for their skin complexions, were identical in every respect, meeting for the first time!! The fact neither parties could understand the other would have made the drama surrounding the extraordinary meeting of humans even more intense.

Following the shock, came the realisation that, despite the differing skin colours and the language barriers, they were all humans after all.

Soon both parties got down to business. In due time they traded for their mutual benefit. Through the process of silent barter, the foreigners and natives traded with each other. The natives had something the newcomers wanted – gold. The newcomers had brought something the natives needed – clothes guns, and other manufactured good.

If only the newcomers would restrict themselves in the trade in wares; but they wouldn't! In due course, trade was extended into the trade in humans. So began the transatlantic slave trade, which was to last for over 400 years. Though figures are not precise, it is estimated that around 12–13 million Africans were sold during the period. Though some ended up in Europe, the vast majority were shipped across the Atlantic to North and South America. The transatlantic slave trade was officially abolished on 1 January 1808.

Not only did the trade result in the depletion of the African population, it also created the conditions for the subsequent colonial conquest of Africa by the European powers.

It was during the period of European involvement in Africa that the terms "black" and "white" to describe humans were invented.

The first recorded reference to Europeans as "white" was in the play *The Triumphs of Truth*, by the English playwright Thomas Middleton. Performed for the first time on 29 October 1613, a character depicting an African king looked upon the English audience and declared: "I see amazement set upon the faces/Of these white people, wond'rings and strange gazes."

The concept of the "white" European, at least as far as any written record bears witness, was thus born. Put in other words, the concept of the "white" person is only a little over 400 years old.

If only the matter had ended there! But no – whiteness would only make sense if posed next to blackness. Where could one invent blackness, but in the "dark" African continent! Thus every resident of that continent, from the pale-coloured Igbo of Nigeria to the darkest brown coloured Masai of Kenya, were all dumped in the black pot of blackness!

One might have allowed the matter to rest – but for the negative connotations.

A child born into the world by African parents has a huge disadvantage to start with, even if his skin is as light coloured as an Igbo of Nigeria. As everyone is calling them black, a colour associated with all types of evil and negative connotations, they are forced to shoulder the additional burden of the negative association and stigmatisation throughout their lives.

On the other hand, the child born to a European is called white, even though he or she is not actually white, and as white is associated with innocence and purity, they are looked upon more favourably by society.

Should the "black" individual and the "white" individual later appear for an interview, even though they have the same grades, because the individual who is "black" is associated with malice and inferiority and the "white" counterpart with goodness and superiority, the latter stands a better chance of being selected.

In his 1967 essay, "The English Language is My Enemy", the American author, playwright and civil rights activist Ossie Davis, lamented the strongly negative connotations of the word "black" and its synonyms in English.

Well, I don't think the English language per se is his enemy. As I will allude to later in this discourse the association of black to bad things is not unique to the English language – it is also found in several other languages including German. I am mentioning German because it is the only European language apart from English that I am conversant with. Members of the jury may be familiar with connotations in their vernacular and other languages with which they are familiar.

The real enemy is not the English language. In my opinion, the real enemy is the world population that has come to accept the usage of those terms, coined by a human being over 400 years ago, as normal – as part and parcel of everyday language.

I personally ask myself why we have accepted the designation "black" in mainstream language to describe people of Africa descent – those whose skin complexion is as fair as the Igbo of Nigeria – but feel offended by the use of the term "nigger" to describe Africans? The term "nigger" is indeed considered so offensive it is often referred by the euphemism the "N-word". Personally, I also find it offensive to call me black when I am not! Some may recognise a difference between the two designations but, as far as I am concerned, referring to me as black is just as derogatory as calling me nigger!

Ladies and gentlemen of the jury, I ask myself: why should we allow a construct created 400 years ago, at a time when the trade in humans was considered normal, to be officially sanctioned in modern times, in the social media age of the twenty-first century?

Calling me black even though I am chocolate brown coloured, immediately leads to associations. Even if the large majority of humans would not see things that way, still a significant number would be inclined to do just that. So if I happen to be walking on the streets of London, with an English person of my age who perhaps work in security (nothing wrong with that – it is only an illustration), then by virtue of my skin colour the police may be inclined to stop and search me and allow the English fellow to go his way – even if I manged to make it from my impoverished background, forced by poverty to sleep on a mat spread on the bare floor of our dilapidated home, all the way to the prestigious Hanover Medical School in Germany! Ladies and gentlemen of the jury, I hope you are gradually getting an idea as to how far the association with the degraded colour "black" can negatively impact on one's journey through life.

I will return to the matter in my closing statement. For now I want to dedicate myself to something else.

Part two

At home in the global village

2A

Debunking the idea of an "angry black man"

S ome who read or listen to my presentation to the jury might think the whole issue boils down to the case of an "angry black man", an individual who, for reasons best known to himself, has long harboured resentment against Europeans, and who has just taken advantage of the tragic death of Mr George Floyd to fulfil his personal agenda.

Far from it! As I made it known earlier on, as far as I am concerned, I am driven by principles and nothing else. Still, I consider it prudent to provide you, ladies and gentlemen of the jury, with a quick background sketch of me, so as to shed light on my person and let you know the extent to which, over the last few years, I have interacted with, and continue to reach out to, people in all walks of life, including a large number of individuals of European descent.

Indeed since my arrival on the soils of Europe, to be precise in the then West Berlin in May 1982, I have had, and continue to have, several German friends, acquaintances, associates etc. Do you require, ladies and gentlemen of the jury, a reference from my German friends and close acquaintances? I am happy to provide several of them. I can indeed list at least 50 of them. For the sake of space, I will restrict myself only to just two dozen. So here we go ...

Alex, Anette, Angelica, Anna, Antje, Astrid, Barbara, Bernhard, Birgit, Brigitte, Burghard M., Burghard Z., Claudia, Esther, Goetz, Gottfried, Ilse, Ina, Manuela, Norbert, Reinhard, Roland, Sonja, Uwe.

These are not superficial contacts. They are individuals who, if they found me stranded on the streets of a German city, would not hesitate a minute to invite me to their home, and provide me a place to spend the night. Of course the converse is also true. Who then can accuse me of resentment towards people of European decent?

I will now proceed to provide you, ladies and gentlemen of the jury, with a short background account of myself.

I was born into very humble circumstances in the small village of Mpintimpi, situated about 90 miles to the northwest of Accra, Ghana's capital.

A makeshift bathroom served as the "labour ward". Mother had to endure the terrible labour pains with no healthcare professional around to administer pain relief. She was helped by a traditional midwife.

My parents were poor peasants. Indeed, the saying "as poor as the church mouse" aptly applied in their case.

Since this discourse revolves around the issue of skin colour, I want to digress a bit to reveal something about my parents, which is not irrelevant to the theme.

Mother was unusually fair in complexion compared to the general population of the village. Did she acquire her fair colour through the process of bleaching, perhaps? Mother spending money to bleach her skin? Forget it. Even if she could afford it, she wouldn't have done so out of principle (she was strongly against the practice).

How then did she come by her fair skin complexion? I have no idea! It was a predominantly illiterate community, a setting in which births were not recorded. It is superfluous to mention that tracing one's lineage several years back was practically impossible.

Up until recently, I did not give much thought to the fact of mother's light complexion. But then recently, as I pondered the matter, an idea flashed through my mind! Did one of my great-great-great grandmothers perhaps fall prey to the lust of a European slave master? The slave merchants, they were human after all! Confronted with the native beauties – some of whom could today be crowned as Miss Universe if they bothered to take part in the beauty pageantry – could not resist the temptation of the weak flesh. Thus instead of concentrating on the main purpose for which they descended on the west African coast – trade in all sorts of wares including humans – they forced the innocent African beauties to go to bed with them – how can one speak of consent in such a relationship?

In any case, my late mother was fair in complexion; father on his part was dark coloured – one may speak of chocolate coloured.

The coming together of the two hearts resulted in children of varying skin complexions, from dark brown to pale hues.

Indeed out of their eight children – five boys and three girls– two boys and two girls inherited their mother's fair complexion; three boys, including yours truly and one of our sisters, inherited father's dark brown skin colour.

I was born just about the time the Gold Coast gained independence from the British and was renamed Ghana. Though my parents did not have any formal education, the free education policy introduced by the government of the newly independent country worked for me. Free education was not only on paper – those who failed to send their children to school risked prosecution.

There was no primary school at Mpintimpi. We had to attend the Roman Catholic primary school at Nyafoman, a comparatively bigger village about two miles to the north of our settlement. My attendance at the primary school, run on behalf of the state by the Catholic Church offered me the opportunity of seeing a person of European descent for the first time.

The Roman Catholic diocese responsible for the school was located at Nkawkaw, a big town about 20 miles to the north of Nyafoman. Occasionally the Catholic priest stationed there, who we called "father", visited the Catholic church of the village. On such visits a Catholic mass was celebrated; pupils from the upper year groups had to attend.

Beside the Catholic "father", occasionally Catholic "sisters", nurses of the Catholic hospital at Nkawkaw who happened to be driving past Mpintimpi in their VW Microbus, along the road that divided the village into two equal parts, made a stop in the village to purchase fruit, vegetables and other foodstuffs harvested from our farms, and on display on stands by the sides of the road.

The sight of the Europeans in our small village drew the attention of everyone, especially the children. I remember on such occasions running out of our home, which happened to be located along the road, to have a closer look at the "strange" humans. We usually surrounded them shouting on the top of our voices "Oburoni koko kye me kapre" which literally translated means: "red-coloured Europeans, please give me a penny!" That was somewhere in the early 1960s.

My next contact with people of European descent came when I was about 12 years old. An ailment affecting my left ankle led my parents to take me to the Seventh Day Adventist (SDA) hospitals at Atibie about 30 miles to the north to seek medical help

A big leap in my educational journey came when I moved from our village to attend the boarding school at Akim Oda, our district capital. My time at the second tier school offered me further opportunity to interact with people of European descent. The teaching staff of the secondary school was mostly Ghanaian; but a small proportion was made up of expatriates from various parts of the world – other African countries, India, Pakistan, the United States etc.

The expatriate teachers from the United States came as part of the Peace Corps programme. The majority of them returned home at the end of their posting. Not so Mr Thorne, who was head of the Physics Department in our time. During his stay in Ghana he met and married a Ghanaian lady. In the course of time he became what one might describe as an "Africanised American".

From Oda Secondary School, I went on to do my sixth form at Mfantsipim School in Cape Coast, a city located about 90 miles to the west of Accra, Ghana's capital. My cherished goal was to study medicine at the medical school in Accra, Ghana's capital city. But things did not go as I had envisaged and in the end I missed the chance to study medicine in Ghana. Next, I tried to obtain a scholarship to study in the then Soviet Union. (At that time countries in the eastern bloc annually made available several scholarships for students from the developing world.) That attempt also proved futile.

In December 1980, I left Ghana for Nigeria, with the aim of working to obtain my plane ticket to travel to the then West Germany with the hope of realising my goal of studying medicine. Whilst in Nigeria, I found a job as a teacher in a secondary school. In May 1982, I left Nigeria for the then West Berlin where I applied for asylum. After facing several virtually insurmountable hurdles, in October 1984 I matriculated as a first-year student at the Hanover Medical School. After qualifying as a doctor, I practised in Germany for a while, before moving on to the UK in 2006. I am married to Rita, also a native of Ghana. We have three children.

As far as it lies within my remit, I have throughout my life endeavoured to be on good terms with all human beings irrespective of heritage, social status, educational background etc.

Indeed, personally, I refer to myself as a world citizen, a child of the universe enjoying my stay here as long as He who sent me here permits me so to do.

When I interact with other people, I concentrate on the substance of the matter at stake and not on externals. The colour of the skin of the individual? I am not interested. Does the individual look attractive or ugly– it does not bother me! Are they well dressed? I don't mind, I am not a judge in a fashion show! Are they kempt or unkempt? That is their own problem!

I just do not understand why people make such fuss about issues relating to the externals! Integrity, decency, incorruptibility, virtues that make for human progress, which help us live at peace with one another during our short stay on earth, that is what, as far as I am concerned, is worthy of emphasis.

My upbringing, my Christian faith, my extraordinary life journey and finally my profession as a doctor have helped shape my outlook to life.

Talking of my upbringing: very early in life, I had the opportunity to interact with children of different backgrounds.

What may not be clear to others is that Ghana, and for that matter Africa, is made up of myriads of different population groups, each endowed with a different language, culture, traditions etc. Taking Ghana as an example, my research has revealed that there are around 70 different ethnic groups, each speaking a separate language. Even if we consider only the major groups, we can count around ten of them. When it comes to Africa as a whole, there are said to be 1,500–2,000 different languages!

Although there has generally being a peaceful co-existence of the various population groups in Ghana, there are still tensions between some of them.

As is to be expected when people of different ethnic backgrounds live close to one another, there are ethnic tensions, with some considering themselves more superior than others.

Ach! you thought the problem of prejudice is a unique European problem?! Then join me one day on a research tour of my country to investigate the matter!

Our village is located in a part of the country boasting a tropical rain forest. Though global warming has led to some worsening of the climate and, with it, vegetation, at the time I was growing up, the forest was generally regarded as fertile. The fertile land attracted individuals and families from other parts of the country to acquire pieces of farmland.

I belong to the Akan population group. Within a time, groups of Ewes, Gas and Dagbanis came to settle in our midst. It offered me the opportunity to interact with children of other tribes.

Besides my childhood experience, my Christian faith requires of me that I love others as myself and treat them with respect. While not claiming to be the most perfect Christian around, I do my best to live in line with my calling.

My extraordinary life journey has also helped mould my life. I have already made mention of my deprived background. Indeed, I made it all the way from Ghana to medical school in Germany with virtually no monetary resources to begin with. Along the way, I received help from kind-hearted individuals too numerous to list here. Having been the beneficiary of the kindness of others, I feel duty bound, so long as it lies within me, to show kindness and respect to all I came across

Last but not least, I want to mention the influence my training as a doctor has had on my outlook on life and my attitude towards others. Human as they are, doctors are not free from prejudice. But by virtue of our profession we are bound to help those who need our medical help irrespective of their backgrounds.

19

Since it is particularly relevant to this discourse, I want at this stage to bear testimony to the assistance I received from an elderly German family doctor at a very critical point in my life journey.

It happened in mid-1984. The immigration authorities were threatening to deport me back to my native Ghana after my application for asylum had been turned down and all the available legal channels had been exhausted. The only way I could be granted leave to stay was on medical grounds. And, indeed, I had a medical condition. On hearing my situation, my German family doctor hesitated not a second in issuing the required medical certificate.

Mind you, he was a German – a person who did not share my skin colour. But he did the right thing at the right time – and I am eternally grateful that he acted in line with the dictates of his profession and conscience. If everyone assumed a similar attitude in their dealings with one another, ladies and gentlemen of the jury, how much of the hatred and rancour going on in our midst could be overcome?

2B

People of European descent providing for my needs

That leads me, ladies and gentlemen of the jury, to the next phase of my presentation – to narrate in some detail the assistance I received from various individuals of European heritage on my path to medical school. Indeed, without the financial assistance of such individuals I would never have been able to finance my medical education in Germany.

Then, as now, tuition is free in German universities for both citizens and non-citizens. Though they are not charged for teaching/lessons, students have to bear the cost of accommodation, food, books and other miscellaneous costs associated with their studies.

At the time I began my studies, it was generally held that students required around 700 German marks (about 360 euros) monthly to sustain themselves. Based on that figure, I had at the outset enough money to last me barely three months.

For the most part of the period of my study, I relied almost entirely on the financial assistance provided by my German friends and acquaintances.

Earlier on, I listed the first names of 24 of my numerous German friends and close associates.

I will now present into some detail the manner several persons of European descent who provided for my needs during my time in Germany, individuals whose indescribable kindness and compassion towards me made me feel incredibly at home in Germany.

Anna is a German lady married to my Ghanaian friend Emmanuel. I will require several pages to list the incredible assistance I received from both.

Gary was the pastor of the American Lutheran Church in Berlin, whose fellowship I shared during my stay in Berlin. Earlier on in my stay I had come across a leaflet of theirs inviting visitors to the city to worship with them. Gary, in particular, and the rest of the congregation, made up mainly of Americans of European descent, were a great help to me during my time in the then divided city.

Charlotte, who is no longer alive, was an elderly German lady who attended the American church in Berlin with her granddaughter, whose father happened to be an American of African descent. Eventually a good friendship developed between the three of us. I still have the memory of the day Charlotte invited me to a shop and presented me with a brand new bike. On countless occasions I was guest in their home. As a poor asylum-seeker in that strange environment, their kindness towards me helped make my difficult situation bearable.

Kurt was the pastor of a German Lutheran church, which happened to be a sister church of the American Lutheran Church. Occasionally we held joint church services. It was during one such meetings that I got to know him.

Kurt played a key role in my university application process by providing a written declaration of financial support in case I gained admission – it was a vital piece of paperwork that I needed to provide before any university would consider my application.

On my admission, Kurt decided, in effect, to put his money where his mouth was and sent regular remittance to support me.

Ilse was a Christian physiotherapist I got to know during my stay in hospital following surgery on my ailing left ankle. The condition first started during my teenage years. It flared up during my first winter in Europe, necessitating surgery. Alone in hospital, far away from home, I found comfort from reading the Bible. That attracted her to me. That meeting came as a blessing. In the end she introduced me to several other German Christians who also became a blessing to me. Ilse assisted me in ways too many to list here.

Rhea, a retired medical doctor, was introduced to me by Ilse. She assisted me in several ways – cash handouts, purchasing me clothes, inviting me to her home for meals etc. When I picked up my studies, she sent regular monthly cash payments.

Ruth and Sabine I got to know from a prayer breakfast group organised by Ilse. Ruth and her daughter Sabine showed me immense favour, on several occasions inviting me home for meals.

Alan and Erika were a middle-aged couple I got to know at the American church in Berlin. On several occasions I was guest in their home, located in a high-end area of the city that boasted exclusive and sumptuous villas.

Friedo was a pastor of a Lutheran Church in Hanover. He happened to be a good acquaintance of Kurt. Kurt established the contact with Friedo on my move from West Berlin to Hanover to begin my medical studies. Not only did Friedo use his influence to get the church to provide me financial assistance, he also regularly invited me home for meals.

My first address in Hanover was in Langenhagen, a suburb of the city. By virtue of that, Friedo connected me to **Gottfried**, who happened to be the superintendent pastor responsible for the Langenhagen area of the German Lutheran Church in the city. Gottfried and his wife Sabine welcomed me wholeheartedly to their home: "You can consider yourself part of our family. In the worst-case scenario, if you are unable to pay your rent, you can come and lodge with us!" they assured me. In the end, Gottfried came up with a plan – he opened an account for me and launched an appeal for help from members of his congregation as well as his numerous acquaintances and associates. From that account he made monthly remittances to me.

Astrid and Karl were a middle-aged couple who attended the Messiah's Church pastored by Friedo. They were marvellously kind to me, inviting me on several occasions to their home for fellowship and meals.

While some of the individuals mentioned above are no longer alive, I still have regular contact with several of those who are still alive.

2C

Friends and close associates from my medical school days and beyond

A s far as I can remember, I was the only African in a year group of about 300 students. I did not feel isolated or abandoned by my German mates. Indeed I got on well with everyone. Even to this day, I have good contacts with a couple of them.

Roland was my room-mate in a doublet students' accommodation. We got on very well. Though our paths separated several years ago, I still have fond memories of our time together.

Cornelia was in my year group. We have maintained regular contact with each other up to this day.

Burghard was a year ahead of me in medical school. We got to know each other in a Bible study group. He wanted to do an elective in Ghana, which I helped organise. During his stay in Ghana, he met some of my extended family members. We have maintained regular contact to this day.

The list of my German friends and close associates at medical school is by no means exhausted. I could indeed keep counting until the cows come home.

I mentioned earlier on that I was the only student with an African background. There were several foreigners from other parts of the globe in our year group. I got on well with everyone including Anoma from Sri Lanka, Pilli from Spain, and **Khosro** from Iran. I lived in the same hostel as Khosro. The medical school library was not far from our hostel. Since each of us preferred studying in the library to doing so in the hostel, our ways crossed on countless occasions. Though our ways have since separated, the good memories I have of our friendship have not. During my medical school days, and also as a doctor, I got to know several nurses and health care personnel. On at least two occasions, I helped arrange for some of them to visit Ghana. During their stay, my brother Ransford took them around the country, including of course visits to my "great" village Mpintimpi.

Charles is a South African of European descent who is now settled in Spain after living in Scotland for a long while. I got to know him when I was looking for a publisher for my first book. Since then, we have maintained good contact with each other, not only by virtue of the professional editing services he provides for my books, but also by virtue of the human touch.

David's carers: Our son David has autism. He has over the years had several carers of European descent. We have got on well with them, not only by virtue of their professional roles but also the human affection.

2D

Photo report: feeling at home in the global village

There is saying that "seeing is believing". To give credence to my claim that I get on well with people of all walks of life and backgrounds, irrespective of colour of skin, religious affiliation, political conviction etc., I am herewith providing the jury a short photo report of the matter to substantiate my case.

**This is a group picture of the teaching staff of the 1981/82 academic year of the Muslim High School in Shagamu, a large town about 50 miles to the north east of Lagos, Nigeria's commercial capital. I am shown in the picture with an arrow pointing to my head. As I mentioned earlier on, I went to Nigeria to work to obtain a plane ticket to Germany. I taught General Science in the junior classes.

Despite its name, the school was secular. Originally a private school owned by a rich Muslim businessman, it had been taken over by the state a few years prior to my arrival there. At that time a nationwide policy of free education for all was introduced. As part of the take-over arrangement, the former proprietor insisted that the school be allowed to maintain its name – and the state agreed.

The Muslim High School was a good example of how people of different religious persuasions and backgrounds could learn and work peacefully side by side. The teaching staff came from all over the world. Apart from Nigerians, there were Ghanaians, Indians and Pakistanis. The great majority of the pupils as well as the teaching staff shared the Muslim faith. Yet hardly any conflict arose on the basis of faith or heritage.

**A picture taken in 1984 at a location not far from the concrete dividing wall of Berlin, showing me and my German Christian sisters after a prayer breakfast.

** On a visit to the home of my German Christian friends in Calw, a town about 20 miles to the west of Stuttgart in 1985.

** A picture taken during a street festival in West Berlin in 1983 showing Pastor Scott, a junior pastor of the American Church in Berlin, and an asylum seeker from Iran, my roommate in the hostel housing asylum-seekers from around the globe. The German ex-serviceman just photo-crashed the shot.

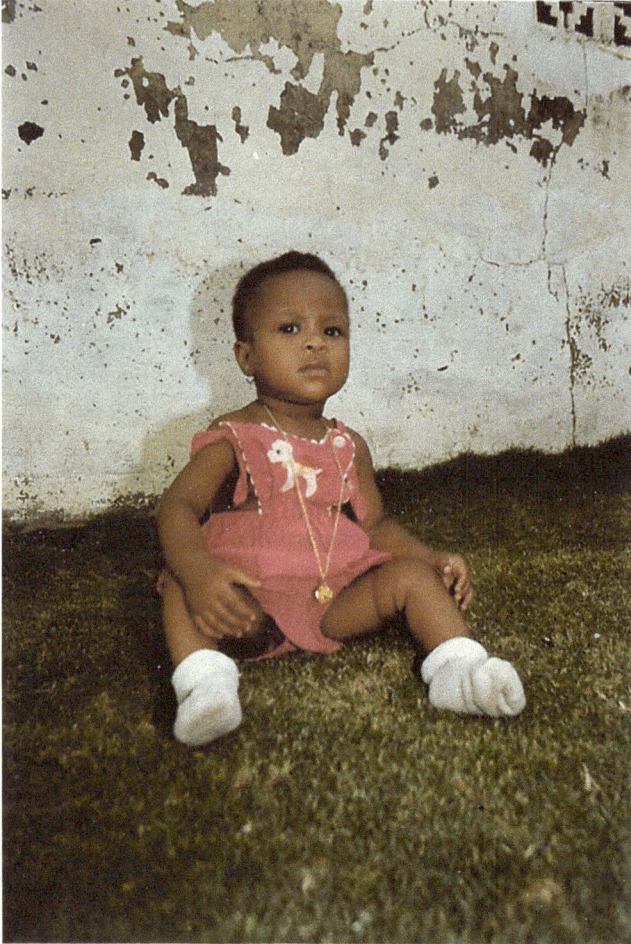

** A picture of my niece, Josephine, the daughter of my brother Thomas. Thomas passed the fair complexion inherited from mother on to her. Is it fair to call her "black"?

** At home with Alan and Erika, a middle-aged couple of European descent of the American Luther Church in Berlin in 1984 – several years on, I still have fond memories of them.

** With Khosro, a fellow student at medical school from Iran. At the same time that he sought to convert me to the Islamic faith, I was praying for his conversion to Christianity! Despite our different religious convictions a close friendship developed between us.

** On not a few occasions, some of my fellow German students as well as nurses from the university hospital accompanied me on trips to Ghana. This and the preceding two pictures depict scenes from some of those trips.

** Enjoying a feast at the home of a fellow member of the American church in Berlin.

** Enjoying a Ghanaian traditional meal of fufu with some of my medical school mates.

** At the birthday party of a German doctor colleague – one could as well describe the meeting as a mini UN summit, with representatives from Asia, Africa and Europe.

** Fellow medical students from Germany on a visit to my village undergoing "training" in carrying children on one's back.

Part three

Thoughts, reflections and essays on issues of colour and diversity

I n the foregoing chapters, I have provided the jury an account of me and my interaction with people of various backgrounds.

I have supported my claim of being a person who usually gets on well with people from different backgrounds with a photo report.

Next I am presenting the jury with articles and essays that I have written that touch on some of the negative perceptions accorded to the colour black, the burden of being born "black" and some of the experiences that I have had as a person of African descent living in Europe. They are presented here in the chronological order in which they were written.

I will also furnish the jury with an article titled 'How "white people" were invented by a playwright in 1613' by Mr Ed Simons , which I find very relevant to the case under review.

3A

The outspoken old lady and the "modern ladies" of our small village (February 1994)

My late mother, bless her! She was fearless, bold, outspoken and forthright when it came to matters of justice, equality, standing on principle; indeed, when it came to what she deemed right.

She was not the type who would let you depart from her presence before giving her opinion about you, to your face; for her, back-biting and destroying others in their absence was out of the question.

As a result of her forthright and plain-spoken nature, other residents used to call her "Ka na wu", meaning in my Twi vernacular "say it as it is – even if it incurs the threat of death"!

At the time I was growing up in our small village, a fashion trend, the practice of skin bleaching, gained popularity in the country. Usually trends in fashion and other issues affecting matters of day-to-day human living, when they begin to take hold in society, are on the whole limited to the urban population. In this particular case, however, the trend gained popularity even among some residents of our small settlement. Imitating their peers in other parts of the country, some young women in our village invested money in so-called miracle-working cosmetics, which their sellers credited with the capability of turning their dark skin colour to a fair-looking one in a matter of days.

As to be expected, some of the illiterate and semi-literates who jumped on the band-wagon were incapable of following the instruction label in regard to the correct use of the "miracle-worker" cosmetic agents. The end-result was that some ended up attaining a non-uniform bleach of their skin. Several spots of their original dark skin persisted side by side with the acquired "fair colour"' of the "modern" ladies walking the streets of our small village.

Mother, in line with her nature, could not keep her mouth shut on such an issue. Whenever she came across such "modern" women on the street she would stop them and say to their faces: "You women of this generation! Why can't you be proud of your natural skin colour! What should I make of this mixture of dark brown, peach and orange you are carrying around!"

"Old woman, please leave us alone!" they replied. "Your time is past. You were born into the Gold Coast. The Gold Coast ceased to exist when we gained our independence from the British in 1957. This is now Ghana. You must learn to accept the fact that we now live in modern times!"

"To hell with your modern times!" she retorted.

3B

The culture shock of an African village boy on excursion to Europe (March 1994)

I spent the time between May 1982 and August 1984 as an asylum-seeker in West Berlin. It was the time of the Cold War. Not only was Berlin divided into East and West, but the whole of Germany and Europe in general was also divided into East and West.

At one point during my stay, I was housed in a hostel overlooking a large forest reserve. On the edge of the forest, not far from where I lived, was a large man-made lake. One thing soon struck me: during the day, particularly on hot days, several cars, as well as people on foot, passed by our house on their way to the lakeside. Out of curiosity, I decided eventually to go there and find out for myself what was happening. I was confronted with the sight of several holidaymakers, some of whom were swimming or playing in the lake; others were engaged in all kinds of games on dry land. A considerable number of those gathered were engaged in something very unfamiliar to me – they simply lay prostrate in the sun on large towels, mats or blankets they had spread out on the green grass. Apart from their bikinis and slips, in the case of the women, and their tight shorts, in the case of their male counterparts, they had nothing else on. Some read from books or magazines, others listened to music from earphones connected to their small music-playing gadgets, whilst others just lay still on their covers, barely moving a limb.

When I returned to the area after several minutes' walk through the forest I noticed a large proportion of those I saw earlier lying in the sun were still there, in just about the same

41

position I had left them! I wondered why they had chosen to spend such a long time in the scorching sun.

At that part of the large forest bordering on the city, everyone I met that day had something on, even if some were, in effect, practically naked! In the course of my stay, my rounds through the forest took me to more remote areas of the green vegetation. There I would be confronted by a sight that someone who grew up in the setting of a small African village could never imagine possible. Before me was gathered a large group of individuals, all of them completely naked – the men, the women as well as the children accompanying them! Some were sunbathing on covers spread on the fields; others were moving around the fields alone or with their partners, friends and children. Yet another group engaged themselves playing various games. None of those present seemed in the least bit bothered by the presence of the intruder!

Initially my assumption was that the scarcity of the sun for most of the year was the only reason that led many people to spend several hours lying almost naked (or actually naked!) in the sun.

In due course, I became aware of the real motive of many who spent several hours lying in the sun – the hope that exposure to the sun's rays would impart a certain degree of tan to their skin. That realisation led me to reflect on human nature.

It is an open secret that some tend to look down on dark African skin. In the light of the aforesaid, I reasoned that those endowed with pale European skin colour would be satisfied with what they have. But that happened not to be the case. They seemed to create the impression that, at the same time that they found the typical African skin too dark, they yearned for a bit more tan for theirs – a middle way between the dark African skin and their light skin.

I mentioned earlier that some individuals in our village invested time and money in an effort to bleach their skin. Now the Europeans, who are already endowed with a fairer skin colour on their part, seemed not to be satisfied with what they have!

Typical humans– we seem never to be satisfied with what we have.

On several occasions during this discourse, I have spoken about the tension that has resulted between population groups by virtue of their varying skin colours. That raises the question – would humans have tolerated each other better had they all been endowed with the same skin colour?

Of course we all know the answer is no. Otherwise brothers and sisters originating from the same parents would not be known, sometimes, to go for each other's throats!

3C

No lobby for the colour black! (April 1995)

Have you sat down to think about the extent to which mankind has gone to degrade the colour black? It really baffles my mind! Someone, please tell me: when did humanity begin to associate the colour black with all that is evil, inferior, negative etc.? I am really keen to know!

Mercy demands that when, for whatever reason, one engages someone in a fight, the moment the opponent is floored one desists from inflicting further suffering to the vanquished by way, for example, of additional blows to the body.

That, obviously does not happen to be the case here. Indeed, even though the colour black has been floored, terribly battered, mercilessly thrashed and is pleading for mercy, no sign of mercy is in sight. Instead it is being ferocious thumped and assaulted further.

A passer-by who came upon the pitiful scene by chance, fearing for his life if he actively, intervened, is left with no other choice than to scream in exasperation "enough is enough!" The intervention falls on deaf ears though – the agonizing hammering of the poor fellow continues unabated!

***

The colour black, what a pity! Because it has no lobby, humanity has decided to associate it with all that is malicious, melancholic, dreadful, ghastly, horrendous, dismal, sorrowful – the list goes on and on and on!

I am no polyglot. Indeed, apart from my mother tongue, the Twi language that is spoken by the Akan population group in my native Ghana, I have managed to acquire what can be described as "satisfactory to good" knowledge of only two other languages. They are namely English, the language of the former colonial masters of the Gold Coast, now Ghana, and German, which I taught myself so as to enable me to fulfil my dream of becoming a doctor.

At some stages in my life, I made attempts at mastering the French and Russian languages; apart from a few words, nothing, however, is left to show for my efforts.

So I am conversant in Twi, English and German.

As far as I know, in Twi, there are hardly any words that directly associate black with evil. That the miserable black still has a negative connotation in the Akan psyche is evidenced by the fact that we usually put on black to mourn our dead.

Concerning the other two European languages I am familiar with, the examples of negative associations with the colour black appears endless. I will first cite a few examples from English.

Black magic: magic involving (supposedly) the invocation of evil spirits for evil purposes.

Black comedy: comedy presenting tragedy in comic terms.

Blackleg: person refusing to join a strike.

Black market: illicit traffic in rationed, prohibited or scarce commodities,

Black mass: travesty of mass in worship of Satan.

Black sheep: a member of a family or group who is regarded as a disgrace, an embarrassment or a shame to the entity.

Black spot: a stretch on a road considered to be prone to accidents.

Black money: income illegally obtained or not declared for tax purposes.

Black day: a day when things go bad.

It must be said that almost all the associations cited above have their direct translation in the German language. For example in German, the equivalent of black sheep is *Schwarze Schafe*; blackmarket is *Schwarzmark*; black money is *Schwarzgeld*.

I am citing other examples of negative association with the colour black in the German language. Some of them have their equivalents in English, others can only be literally translated.

Schwarzer Peter: Black Peter– a scapegoat.

Schwarzarbeit: "black work"– undeclared work, working without a working permit.

Schwarzfahrer: "black traveler" – a fare-dodger.

"Ich sehe schwarz": "I see black" – an idiomatic phrase meaning: "I envision a dire or an undesirable outcome".

Schwarz malerei: painting something black – portraying something or someone as evil.

Schwarz-Weiß-Malerei: Black-and-white portrayal – involving a simple choice between things that are clearly opposite and especially between good and bad or right and wrong.

As already pointed out, it would require volumes to document into details the injustices, abuse, prejudice, maltreatment, discrimination, unfairness – you name them – meted out against poor colour black by humanity.

3D

"Black" Thursday woes (Jan 1997)

I was watching CNN with my barely six-year-old daughter. At one stage there was a report on proceedings on the Tokyo stock exchange. The footage showed scenes from the boisterous trading floor, with several traders running helter-skelter, some gesticulating wildly, some holding their mobile phones close to their ears chatting vigorously with – only God knows whom!

All of a sudden, my little one turned to me:

"Papa, are they crazy" she inquired pointing to the adults on the screen.

"No they aren't!" was my reply.

"What's going on then?" she persisted, the surprise visible in her eyes.

As to be expected of a father, I took pains to explain, from the layman's perspective, what all the hullaballoo was about.

As a doctor, the first thought that came into my mind on seeing the scenes of boisterous activity on the trading floors of the likes of the Tokyo, Frankfurt, London and New York stock exchanges was: I will certainly not recommend this job to anyone with a history of cardiac diseases!

Stock-broking! I learnt the other day that one could make millions of dollars in a single day! All well and good; who can have any issues with money earned within the confines of the law? When things go well for our fellow human beings doing business on the stock exchange markets – hurray, what a wonderful life! Those blessed with the sudden inflow of abundant wealth may have a good time by throwing mega parties, going on cruise holidays, investing in property etc.

Merry, merry, merry living! Nothing wrong with money earned within the confines of the law.

If only matters would stay that way! But no! Let misfortune visit the home of the stockbroker, just as happened in the spectacular crash on Wall Street on 24 October 1929! Oh what a bombshell it was! It is said to have caused tremendous losses to millions.

Guess what happened moments thereafter? Ach! As usual the disgraceful, shameful, unworthy colour black became the scapegoat. Before long, the whole world was speaking of the worst day in the annals of the history of the stock exchange as "Black Thursday". More than nine decades on, the world has not forgotten the colour black for causing the horrendous Black Thursday on Wall Street – an event that would usher in the Greatest Depression of all time!

3E

The most rewarding experience of my medical training (August 1998)

I did my medical training in Germany. As part of the training, I needed to do electives with family doctors or with the practice of a doctor in the community. I had difficulty finding a placement.

In the first place, it was in the early 1990s. Germany had produced junior doctors in abundance. One spoke in German of the *Ärzteschwemme* (literally translated as a "flood of doctors").

Next was my African background. One can imagine a potential employer tending to give preference to German applicants under the prevailing conditions.

After several of my applications had been turned down, I was delighted when I was at last called for an interview. The potential employer had a single-person run practice in a small town about an hour's drive from Hanover.

He did not make a decision on the day of the interview. Instead he asked me to give him a few days to ponder the matter. But a few days later I received a call from him. He had decided to offer me the chance to do the training with him. One can imagine how delighted I was at the opportunity to resume my post-graduate training.

Just as I was making the necessary preparations to take up my position, I got a call from him that unsettled me for some time. My potential employer told me his wife had raised concern regarding the prospect of a dark-skinned person working in the practice. Since it was a small village, she was concerned that I could get into difficulty with the patients.

My potential employer admitted he did not have any issues with my ethnicity, but I should give him some time to seek the opinion of the rest of the team as well as some of his patients.

For a while I was unsettled. Well the matter was beyond my control – I could only wait. A few days later I got a call from him. After thoughtful consideration with his wife, they had agreed to uphold his initial decision to offer me the job. I was delighted they had allowed their convictions to prevail over their fears.

To be fair to them, it was an incredibly bold decision on their part. Residents in a city like Hanover where I resided, who were more likely to come into contact with Africans on quite a regular basis on their streets, could feel comfortable in their presence. This was, however, a remote village in the German countryside, where hardly anyone had had any interaction with a person of my heritage.

It was therefore legitimate on their part to entertain reservations as to whether their patients, especially the elderly among them, would feel comfortable in my presence.

In the end I assumed my position. I tended to leave home each Monday morning and return for the weekend. After a short "getting to know each other period", I quickly settled down in the new environment. Soon I became fully integrated into the practice routine. At no point did I sense being discriminated against, either by the staff or patients.

Apart from seeing patients in the surgery, I was required to visit the elderly who were too frail to visit the surgery. And it was this last group of patients who made my work very fulfilling. The large proportion of them lived in isolation – either as elderly couples or on their own. Their children had grown up and left them to search of work in larger towns and cities. They came round to visit only on important occasions, such as a birthday. For most of the rest of the time, the old were left alone.

So, one can imagine how delighted they were about the weekly visit of their doctor. Some would have wished I spent more time with them than the allotted, just conversing with them. Indeed, whenever my schedule permitted, I did just that.

In the end, I became one of the favourite members of the team, not only among staff members but also my patients. It was indeed with a heavy heart that I bid goodbye not only to my lovely team members but also to my adoring patients.

It was without doubt, one of the most rewarding part of my medical training.

In the end a good friendship developed between my family and that of my former boss. Long after I had left, we exchanged greetings. Though the contact has become rarer in recent years, I look back with much joy to my days working in the small German town. The insight I gained from my experience working in that small community, the only African among Germans, many of whom had, without doubt, prior to my arrival, never interacted with anyone of my background, is that humans are humans everywhere. Reaching out to others, getting to know each other, respecting each other as fellow human beings – these are all that is required to break down some of the prejudices, barriers, ill-feelings etc. we harbour for each other – which, to a large degree, is based on preconceived ideas and thoughts that are often ungrounded and baseless.

3F

400 years of black and white (April 1999)

In an ideal world populated by ideal beings who think rationally all the time, one would expect such beings to place emphasis on the issues that unite them, that binds them together as human beings. There are indeed numerous issues of common interest.

In the first place, each and every one of us needs oxygen to survive. From the most mighty to the commoner, take oxygen from us and nobody would survive past a few minutes. Next on the list of the essentials is water, followed by food.

We also face a common enemies – diseases of various kinds, brought about by various agents and factors.

So in an ideal world one would expect that mankind would join forces to secure an adequate supply of the essentials needed for our survival and fight the common diseases that threaten us.

But instead we tend to concentrate on our differences – of religion, of political ideology, of economic ideology, of national identity etc. As if the headaches brought about by the differences touched upon were not enough!

A little over 400 years ago, we invented yet another sources of rancour and division – the categorising of humans into black and white.

Though the idea of black and white humans is imaginary, a fantasy, since there are indeed no white and black humans beings in the real sense of the word, the categorisation has directly and indirectly led to conflicts too numerous to count.

3G

"Black" accounts made by "white" perpetrators (June 1999)

I n Germany there are two major parties in the country – the Christian Democratic Union (CDU), aka the Conservatives, and the Social Democratic Party (SPD), aka the Social Democrats.

Between 1982 and 1998 the country was ruled by the CDU. But the general election of 1998 brought the opposition Social Democrats to power.

Barely a year after the change of power, it was discovered that, during the reign of the CDU, over a considerable period of time they contravened the laws on party financing by keeping secret overseas accounts.

As was to be expected, the scandal occupied the populace for a while. All of a sudden almost everybody was talking about the "black" accounts of the CDU! Why "black accounts" and not "illegal account"? I was furious. Why behave so unfairly to the innocent colour black?

For the sake of fairness they should have been talking about "white" accounts in line with the prevailing system of classification of God´s children. After all, the people involved in the illegal activity were all Europeans, the banks involved in the secret accounts where the accounts were kept were situated in Europe – and everyone knows that in line with the prevailing system of classification of God´s children, Europeans are "white"!

No, that wouldn't be the case! Instead, all of a sudden, everyone was referring to "black" accounts. I was expecting the more serious media outlets to abide by the principle of neutrality and talk about "illegal accounts". I was disappointed, for they also kept repeating the "black" accounts chorus!

3H

Colourless blood groups (2003)

B lood groups! The issue of the distribution of blood groups among humans is really intriguing. Science, medical science to be specific, has established that basically there are four types of blood – groups A, B, AB and O. One can sub classify the groups into RhD positive and RhD negative. This account is certainly no dissertation for a doctorate degree in medicine, so I want to leave it with the basics – I shall stick to the basic categorisation into the four groups already referred to.

The fascinating, astonishing aspect of the four types of blood groups is the fact that they are randomly distributed among humans. They are indeed distributed in a manner that permeates any imaginable barrier known to mankind – skin colour, national borders, social standing, one's standing on the academic ladder etc.

Put another way, the distribution of the four main types of human blood has no regard to one's skin colour, social status, educational background, political affinity, religious beliefs, nationality etc.

I personally do not cease to give thanks to the Almighty God for the way he did things, the same type of blood flowing through the veins of the royals as well as the commoner.

During my secondary school days, I was baffled when I came across the term "the blue blood of royals" in some novels I read. How could anyone's blood be blue? I wondered! Of course, now I am advanced enough in my knowledge to know the truth of the matter.

Oh how soothing, the knowledge that the distribution of blood groups does not discriminate between a commoner and a royal! A person belonging to the lower caste in India could, for example, be endowed with the same type of blood group as a member of the upper caste in that society. A homeless individual sleeping rough under a bridge in New York under the biting cold winter temperatures may well be endowed with the same kind of blood as the Hollywood star literally swimming in abundant riches in a settlement in the neighbourhood of the Hollywood Hills.

A beautiful top model, a celebrity a la superlative, a star among stars, should she get into an emergency situation requiring urgent blood transfusion, could well be saved by the blood of one of the most ugly and deprived individuals on earth!

I do not want anyone to read any politics into this – the fact remains that a Palestinian living in East Jerusalem could possess the same blood group as his Jewish counterpart in the western part of the holy city!

And a person of African descent could as well donate blood to their European siblings. (I do not want to apologize for the use of the word sibling in this context – the fact that we are all part of the human family, I hope, has become clear to all.)

Before I leave the stage, I want to present the case of two neighbours I once heard about. One of them is of African descent and a staunch member of the Black Panthers. The other is a European, a devoted member of White Supremacy Club. The two have been at logger-heads for decades!

The Black Panther has made it a habit each morning to swear aloud in front of his bathroom mirror: "So long as I have breath in my body, I will never exchange a word with that chunk of bones!!" pointing in the direction of the neighbour.

At about the same time, the White Supremacist, having woken up from a deep sleep, is tidying up in the bathroom and swearing to send the dirty fellow across the street behind bars at the least opportunity.

As a neutral person in the matter, I do ask myself: has either of them sat down to consider this – a situation could arise during which the blood flowing in their veins could be the only available to save the other from threatening death! To that, each of them might respond: "No never! Under no circumstances would I consent for the blood of that devil to be transfused into my body!"

Well, so long as they are conscious, they could probably resist. I don´t know the laws existing in their country. But one thing I am aware of is that, generally, irrespective of where one lives, once one becomes unconscious, the universal law of the "best interest" takes effect, permitting doctors to do what they think to be the right thing in the situation to save the life of an individual.

The provision is based on the assumption that if the affected happened to be conscious they would have accepted the life-saving measure.

Would either of the two bitterly antagonistic, belligerent individuals, who profited from the blood of the other, on regaining consciousness request the doctors to draw out the blood and return it to the hated neighbour?!

31

Those who consider the Germans more racist than the English (2007)

I arrived in Germany in 1982. I matriculated at the Medizinishe Hochshule Hannover (MHH) in 1984. After qualifying as a doctor and working in various German hospitals and in primary care as a family doctor, I moved to the UK in 2006.

Not long after my arrival in the UK, I got to know a Nigerian doctor. During the break we engaged in conversation. He revealed that he came to the UK to do his postgraduate training after completing his basic training in Nigeria.

Initially, he thought I had followed a similar path – basic training in Ghana followed by postgraduate training in the UK. When I let him know that I did all my training in Germany, he was taken aback.

"How did you manage to study in the German language?".

"Well, it was a tough call. I had to put in the maximum effort to acquire the knowledge. Don't take me to be someone who speaks most perfect German though!"

"Tell me, how did you get on with the Germans. I understand they are racist!"

"Who told you?"

"Well, that is the general impression we get here."

"Well, personally, I felt at home. I have several German friends. Indeed, I have lost count of my German friends and acquaintances. On countless occasions I was invited home for meals by my numerous German friends and associates."

"Germans inviting you home for meals?! That is something beyond my imagination!"

"Why so?"

"I have been here in England for several years, but no English colleague has invited me to their home!"

"Well, I felt so much at home by virtue of the kindness shown me by my German friends during my stay in West Berlin, I used to call Berlin my second home!"

"Really!"

"Yes, indeed."

There followed a short silence, which was then broken by me.

"I want to tell you the impression I gained living in both Germany and the UK."

"Go ahead!"

"Please take it as something subjective, from my own point of view. Others may disagree with me. Based on my experience, this is what I think about the Germans and the English. I find the Germans forthright. If they don't like you, they tell you to your face. They don't allow you to leave them only to express their dislike of you in your absence."

"Oh, then they are just the opposite to the English. They will pretend to like you, won't say anything in your presence. It is only when you are gone that they say it", my friend remarked.

"Well, you have taken the words out of my mouth!" I added. "That probably explains why you think the Germans are more racist than the English! I personally like it when they tell you to your face – then I know where I stand. That is what the Germans do. But once they discover you to be honest in your ways, they accept you wholeheartedly. That was my experience".

I thought that would be the last time I would engage in such a conversation with a person of African descent resident in the UK. But no! Indeed, not very long after engaging in that conversation with my doctor colleague, I had a similar conversation with my accountant, a native of Ghana. It would follow further conversations with others of my background living in the UK.

I began to wonder. How did they gain that impression? Through the UK press? Through books? Through conversations? Have the English, cunningly one might say, managed to conceal their racist tendencies towards the African population in their midst?

***

(2020 addition)

Whether the Germans or the French or the British or any other European population group can be regarded as more racist towards Africans than the average European population is not the issue at stake now. What this campaign is demanding to begin with is an end to the practice of designating humans as "black" and "white", at least in official usage.

The more complex task of tackling other issues, such as stereotyping and stigmatising, as evident from the conversation with my African friends concerning the Germans, can follow thereafter.

3J

False generalisations (2008)

The issue of false generalization is a common human trait. For example, in our culture – I don't know how it came to be – residents seem to consider Western industrialised countries, which we usually term as Aburokyire, as a kind of paradise on earth.

In the minds of many people at home, the term Aburokyire could as well be interchanged with terms like "great wealth", "paradise on earth", "luxury" and "enjoyment without end", etc. That fact has in turn led to illogical presumptions, conclusions, inferences, etc., in the minds of many individuals at home. This assumption led them to think that whoever lives in such societies is wealthy. Previously we associated only Europeans who came to us as wealthy.

Now, a new factor has entered the equation – those of our people who have travelled to settle in industrialised societies. Since everyone living there is wealthy, they expect us to become rich overnight.

The writer of this lines faces a double dose of this assumption! For not only are residents of the West presumed to be rich, but also professionals such as doctors, lawyers, architects, are also generally looked upon by society everywhere to be wealthy. I am not only in the industrialised West, but I am also a doctor! But I still have to pay my bills and other expenses.

That leads me back to the issue at stake. Now it is no secret that in almost every language, black is associated with evil and all that is bad; while on the other side, white is associated with innocence. Because the colour black depicts evil and inferiority and white superiority, a "white" individual may be inclined to look down upon a "black" individual. That is why I am calling for an end to such associations.

3K

Evil from within and not from without (2020)

My life journey took me from my small village of Mpintimpi, to our district capital Akim Oda, then to Cape Coast. From there I moved on to Nigeria. After a short transit stay in the then East Berlin, I moved on to West Berlin and then West Germany.

After spending a little over 20 years in Germany, I moved to the UK, where I have been resident for the past 14 years. I have been to Belgium, Holland and France, and have also made a stop-over in Lisbon on a flight from London to Accra. Though I did not get out of the airport building, I had a glimpse of what humans there looked like. I have travelled too to the US, Israel and South Africa.

I have practised medicine in Europe, mainly in Germany and the UK. I have also treated patients as a medical student in Ghana.

By virtue of practising medicine in Europe, and in particular the UK, I have met humans of practically any known skin colour on earth.

Never during my journeys through the world, or during my medical practice, have I ever encountered a black or white coloured human being. So, fellow human beings, aka *Homo sapiens*, why all the talk about black and white humans?

Another insight that I have gained by virtue of working as a prison doctor for over 12 years in the UK – the colour of one's skin has no influence on how much the depraved human mind can sink into evil.

Indeed I have seen people of European descent commit the most horrible types of crime the depraved human mind can think of– including murder, rape, child sex abuse... you can go on naming them. And that is true of people of Africa descent, as well as Arabic, Middle Eastern etc.

I do not want to turn this discourse into a sermon, but the bottom line is that evil, and the tendency to commit evil crime, does not depend on the skin colour.

We can go back into the history of the last 100 years and ponder the evil, horrific and despicable deeds of the likes of Adolf Hitler, Pol Pot and Idi Amin to find ample evidence of the fact I am trying to convey.

3L

A head-scratching experience (February 2020)

I encountered the following classification of ethnic groups in the UK on a UK government official website:

- White
  - English / Welsh / Scottish / Northern Irish / British
  - Irish
  - Gypsy or Irish Traveller
  - Any other White background
- Mixed / Multiple ethnic groups
  - White and Black Caribbean
  - White and Black African
  - White and Asian
  - Any other Mixed / Multiple ethnic background
- Asian / Asian British
  - Indian
  - Pakistani
  - Bangladeshi
  - Chinese
  - Any other Asian background
- Black / African / Caribbean / Black British
  - African
  - Caribbean
  - Any other Black / African / Caribbean background

- Other ethnic group
    - Arab
    - Any other ethnic group

Going through the list led me to say to myself – my goodness, just consider where all the division of humans into race, ethnicity, tribes etc. has led us!

As I pondered further on the matter, I put to myself the question: how based on the classification should I categorise a child born to a white English and white Scottish couple?

What about those born to a couple with the following classification: "Any other Asian background" and "Multiple ethnic background"?

Finally, can someone please help me place a child born to a couple of a white Gypsy and a multiple ethnic background into the appropriate population group!

3M

No race but the human race (March 2020)

I recently encountered the word "bi-racial".
Bi-racial? What, for God's sake, does that mean? I wondered.
So I decided to google the term. This approximately is what I got– children born to individuals of two races.

That explanation, or call it definition, prompted me to have a closer look at the term race. This is the insight I gained concerning race as applied to humans. I learnt that in the biogenetic sense, there is one and only one race, namely the human race.

In recent times, however, I was told the term has been expanded to encompass artificial constructs such as the "white" European and "black" African races!

Staying with the term "biracial" as now artificially constructed. Once upon a time, a "bi-racial" prince from the marriage of the white British and black British races was strolling through a field. Just about the same time, another bi-racial, an attractive princess, a product of a marriage between a Japanese princess and an Arabian prince, was walking her dog in the park.

Just then the eyes of both individuals met. One may perhaps assume a form of biomagnetic phenomena or force emanating from each, serving to attract one to the other. Others may choose to term it love on first sight

Whatever the case, the fact remains that the two developed such fondness for each other that it led the wedding bells of the village church to start ringing loud and clear just a few weeks after the fateful meeting. And barely 12 months after the joyful occasion, they gave birth to a sweet little baby.

"You better say they gave birth to a quadracial child!" a good friend of mine with knowledge in such matters just whispered into my ears.

"Quadracial? my goodness, I have never heard of the term!"

"Well, you better keep reading to keep abreast with the times. We do indeed live in a world in which terminologies keeps evolving and developing!" my friend pointed out to me.

"Okay, thanks for the advice good friend. I know you are an expert in such matters. Before I do the training you have recommended, can you please let me know how I should I refer to a baby born to a quadracial couple?"

"I must confess, I have been caught on the backfoot! I will research the matter and get back to you as soon as I know!"

Tsk! My friend is not after all the guru in the matter of racial categorisation I had thought him to be!

3N

The woes of a chocolate brown fellow under coronavirus lockdown! (April 2020)

I am sat in front of my laptop. It is lockdown in the UK and in many other parts of the world. Just imagine it, a virus has caused a shut down. So I am in virtual house arrest.

I am getting crazy. In order to avoid a situation where my head will literally explode from the tension that has built up in me, I decided to just switch on my laptop and write anything that comes to mind – just to while away the time. Plenty of time has come my way by virtue of the naughty coronavirus!

Was it due to the tension that had built in me? I don't know. But for whatever reason, I decided to take a closer look at both of my palms.

Just then, it began to dawn on me in the most powerful of terms that the colour of my palms, and for that matter those of the soles of my feet, are different from the rest of my body!

Wait a moment, I heard a voice in me tell me – you have been living with this condition for almost 60 years, why then are you making a hullabaloo about the matter now?

At that moment it occurred to me that should the coronavirus lockdown continue for a while, I stood a real danger of ending up on a psychiatrist ward!

So, if my palms and soles are peach, what then is the colour of the rest of my skin? I should rather call on experts on the matter of skin colour designation for help in the matter.

While not claiming to be an expert in the matter, one thing that is beyond dispute is the fact that the colour of my skin is not black! No, black I am not. Black indeed is the colour of the laptop in front of me. In truth, my skin is a bit fairer than the black laptop in front of me.

"So, tell us at long last, you big-mouthed and big-headed bloke from little Mpintimpi, you who, up till the age of 15, was unable to differentiate between the right and left parts of his footwear!" I hear someone laughing mockingly at the other end of the road on hearing that.

"Hey, good friend, who was born into opulence and affluence! How do you expect me to know the difference when abject poverty forced me to resort to my ' natural' pairs of shoes in rain or shine?!"

Let me get back to where I left off before I get completely derailed. So, what is the colour of my skin? Ach, I think it looks just like the piece of chocolate I was presented with by a work colleague not long ago. I refuse however to name the brand in order not to be accused of trying to advertise someone else's product!

So, friend, you better call me chocolate brown or, in case you forget, just an African!

30

Black, white and tasty pizza (1 June 2020)

H ello, fellow human beings. Please pay attention as I share with you a pleasant experience I had on the very first day of June, in the "year of the coronavirus", 2020.

Before I proceed, I want to declare that I am a person of African descent.

The reason, why I have decided to make that known to the rest of the world is not accidental. I do not want to reveal further details now – they will become clear at the end of the narration.

So here we go.

It was Monday 1 June 2020, around 10:30pm, UK time. I had worked much of the day (from 9am till 10pm) as a doctor on the healthcare unit of a prison in a city about 90 minutes' drive from my home. I had been sent there by my agency. Since I was due to work a similar session the next day, I decided to stay in a hotel instead of driving home.

I was hungry; I had not eaten much during the day due to the busy session. On my way to the hotel, I made a detour through the centre of town to order a take-away.

As I drove along, I turned on the radio and tuned in to BBC radio. They were reading the 10pm news bulletin. Much of it revolved around the tragic death of George Floyd and the demonstrations it had triggered in several places in the US and across the globe.

Eventually I pulled my car to a stop near a fast food restaurant. The first instruction I received on entering was on the issue of social distancing (I had forgetfully drawn quite close to the person ahead of me in the queue). "Welcome to the post-coronavirus world", I murmured.

What I have so far not mentioned is that I had been working in the town for a while. Usually I ordered from a Chinese restaurant. The practice was to order half an hour before the close of my duty. When I did so that particular night, the system told me the shop was closed, which I later found out to be a technical hitch.

After being in the queue a few minutes, I was handed a menu. Let me stress the fact, I was entering the shop for the first time and so was not familiar with their menu.

Was it because I was not familiar with the menu? Was it because tiredness had led to a loss of concentration on my part? In any case, I misread the menu. Initially I thought I had ordered two small portions of chips plus two portions of salad to go with it. As it turned out, I had actually paid for two pizzas and two portions of chips!

The error became apparent to me when, after waiting several minutes to be served, I decided to approach the assistant to find out what was causing the delay.

"You ordered two pizzas and two chips. Please be aware that we need some time to prepare them."

"Two pizzas and two portions of chips?! How do you expect me to eat that much food on my own!"

"Sorry, it is too late to cancel; we have already started preparing the order".

"Never mind; you keep the money and serve me one portion of each."

"What should we do with the remainder?"

"You eat it yourself, or give it to someone else!"

"No, we are not hungry; you have ordered them – you take them."

My goodness, what am I going to do with such an abundance of food?! I wondered. The thought of ending up having to throw part of the order away filled me with anger.

Still confused as to what to do with the surplus food, I collected the order and stepped out of the building. I had barely taken a few steps in the direction of my vehicle when two shabbily dressed young men – some may call them junkies – who had been hanging around the building approached me.

"Sir, can you please give us some money for food? We are hungry!"

"You don't need to buy anything; I have something for you.!"

"What?"

"Freshly prepared pizza and chips!" So saying I reached into the paper bag containing the order, removed the bigger of the two pizzas and a portion of the chips and handed it to them.

"Good man! God bless you, fellow!" they said, as if with one voice

"Thanks; I need all the blessing that I can get!" I replied and walked away.

How delighted I was! Indeed the thought of being able to share my food with one of my own, my fellow human beings, instead of throwing it away filled my heart with great joy.

As I drove on, I reflected on my chance meeting with the two gentlemen. They were European, I was African. We were all hungry, yearning for food to still our hunger. I was delighted at the opportunity to help them; they were no doubt grateful for the help from a fellow human being.

As I enjoyed my pizza, I pondered the matter. If humanity would concentrate on what we share in common, instead of dwelling on the differences, even though we might not be able to build a heaven on earth, how many conflicts could be avoided?! If we could learn to bear each other irrespective of the skin colour we are endowed with, instead of waste our energies on highlighting our differences, how many conflicts stirred by racial prejudice would we avoid?

3P

The joy of a lone African in an "all-white" church (15 June 2020)

I was horrified to watch the brutal killing of the US citizen George Floyd by a fellow citizen, a police officer, on the streets of Minneapolis on Monday 25 May 2020.

At the same time that I decry the abhorrent deeds of a police officer of European descent against an individual of African descent, I think it will be catastrophic to sterilise the matter into a kind of racial war between Europeans and Africans.

Even as I write, there are millions of Europeans and Africans enjoying life together as couples, working colleagues, humanitarian workers etc.

There are, indeed, problems between sections of both communities. We should, however, learn to put matters in the right perspective.

In this regard, I want to share with the global community the incredible kindness and favours I received from Americans of European descent, members of the American Lutheran Church in Berlin, where I worshipped during my stay in the then divided Berlin between 1982 and 1984.

I had arrived there as an asylum-seeker. Handicapped by my lack of knowledge of the German language, I was on the lookout for an English-speaking church to worship with.

On a stroll through the centre of the city., my attention was drawn to a tall Victorian-style church building, partly destroyed at the top.

It happened to be an attraction, for there were considerable comings and goings into the building by sightseers who had taken advantage of the good weather to stroll the streets. Out of curiosity, I joined the queue of those wishing to enter the building.

Once inside the building, I spotted a table with bunches of leaflets. One of them happened to be from the America Lutheran church in Berlin. English-speaking visitors to the city were being invited to join them in Sunday worship. I did not hesitate in calling the number. Eventually, Gary, the pastor directed me to the church. I worshipped with them the following Sunday.

As it turned out, I was the only person of African descent worshipping with them. I was heartily welcomed by the congregation. Eventually, I became a member. Later I introduced several other Ghanaian asylum-seekers to the church. In the end, it became quite well known to the Ghanaian refugee community in Berlin.

I spent 18 months in West Berlin before moving to Hanover to study medicine. Not only did I enjoy the company of the congregation. When I gained admission to study medicine, I received financial support from them too. Even to this day, I recall the wonderful brand-new bike presented to me by one of the members.

It is utopic to think we can completely eradicate racial prejudice and hatred from the surface of an imperfect world. It is important, however, that we do the little we can to promote understanding among mankind.

3Q

The nightmare of colourless drug addicts (June 2020)

I have worked over 12 years as a prison doctor in the UK. I do not want to consult any official statistics on the matter. Instead I want my statement to be based on my own experience. A considerable number of the prison population, in both male and female prisons, are serving sentences for drug-related crimes.

There are broadly three categories. There are those who sell or supply drugs without themselves being addicted to them. They regard it as a kind of business, though they are certainly profiting from the woes and miseries of others.

The second group of individuals engaged with drugs are addicted to the substances; they sell drugs to help them pay for their own addiction.

The final group of drug users that I encounter in prison are addicted to various kinds of substances. They are forced to commit other crimes to finance their addiction.

It is beyond the realm of this discourse to delve in any detail into the issue of crime and prison life. But before I leave this explosive field, I want to dwell briefly on one group of offenders, namely the frequent offenders or reoffenders. They are, in the main, drug addicts. Their addiction brings with it a chain of problems too numerous to list here. Most importantly, hardly any of them are able to pay to maintain a fixed abode. To such individuals, prison has become a kind of home. Release them into the community, and they deliberately commit crime with the main intention of being sent back to prison – their "home" as it were!

I have become so familiar with them, the "ins and outs" of the prison where I have been working for the last several months.

"Back again?" I begin on seeing them in the reception clinic where new arrivals are first screened for various health conditions, including their drug habits.

"Yes, Doc! What else do you expect? Nowhere to live!"

Aware of the case I was about to present to the world jury, during a recent session in prison I decided to pick a few cases at random in order to make my point. So here we go.

***

The first case I am presenting involved a 35-year-old English man. When I first saw him, I took him for a 50-year-old – his drug habit had had a telling effect on him, leading to obvious signs of premature aging. He was in a terrible and pathetic state. It was a Monday and he had been in police custody since Friday.

He told me he was injecting at least £100 worth of heroin, which is ten "bags" of street heroin. One bag is usually 0.1 gram, which means he was injecting around 1 gram of heroin daily. Deprived of heroin for almost three days, he was displaying obvious signs of withdrawal. He needed medical help to relieve his suffering. I had to prescribe him methadone, a synthetic opioid drug that is used in the treatment of heroin and opiate drug-withdrawal symptoms.

I knew it was only tackling the symptoms and not the cause of the problem. The root cause was for him to overcome his addiction. Until that happened, he was a prisoner to his habit, his heroin addictive habit.

***

Next to be seen was a 61-year-old man of both African and European heritage; others may choose to call him a bi-racial individual. I am not comfortable in the use of such designation. His problem was similar to that of the previous individual. He was addicted to opiates and needed methadone to avert withdrawal symptoms.

At 61, he was one of the oldest inmate I had seen with drug issues for a long time. Unfortunately, a good deal never make it to an age that, in their group, can be described as "very advanced". Many die before attaining such an age – directly from the effects as well as indirectly.

***

Whether by accident or design, the next person I saw for the evening best closes the circle on the selected cases suited for our present discussion.

She was a female patient, an African, with what can be described as the darkest brown skin colour. 39 years of age and from east Africa, she was also addicted to heroin and, as in most cases, had been sent to prison on drug-related charges.

***

Three individuals – a European, an African and a person of both African and European heritage. And one major problem – addiction to drugs!

Male, female, "black", "white", high class social standing, low class social standing – all hijacked by their addition to drugs!

Where then is the "supremacy" some claim for themselves and the artificial construct they refer to as "race"

3R

Nasty corona knows no colour (June 2020)

It is really becoming embarrassing, it borders on paranoia! In the spirit of tit for tat, in response to the "Black Lives Matter" campaign, some fans of the English football club Burnley organised a "White Lives Matter Burnley" stunt, in which an aircraft towed a banner bearing the words over the Etihad stadium in Manchester during the Premier League match between Manchester City and Burnley on Monday 22 June 2020.

The impression is being created that there is a "racial war" going on between people of African descent, designated "blacks", and those of European descent, the "whites". I find the whole matter demeaning and shaming; a kind of child's play.

Often, I ask myself, why has this conflict between Africans and Europeans played out before the world public for generations? It seems to portray a fact, which is erroneous, that people of other heritage – Indian, Chinese, Japanese, Middle Eastern – do not harbour degrees of prejudice among each other and also toward Africans.

The fact remains, however, that whatever tension there is between population groups, it does not spill into the public domain as frequently as is the case with "blacks" and "whites".

Without doubt there have been conflicts and tensions between other population groups. I have in mind the perennial, enduring conflict between Israel on the one hand and the Palestinians on the other. But I think it is fair to say that that has nothing to do with the colour of skin, but rather with more complex socio-political issues. Anyway, that is how I see the matter. Others may disagree with me.

The issue of "black" and "white" humans – my goodness! At the end of the day, that we belong to a biogenetically identical human race – not white, black, brown, yellow or whatever colours we want to describe human beings – is evident from the coronavirus pandemics that is raging through the world. That alone should have called an end to the discussions on race, of others being of other races.

It is superfluous to mention here that coronavirus is able to infiltrate our lungs, hijack our lungs, for its own selfish means, to replicate itself, notwithstanding the colour of our skin. Indeed the bitter reality is that, in the worst-case scenario, nasty coronavirus could send us to our graves irrespective of the colour of our skin!

3S

'How 'white people' were invented by a playwright in 1613'

The Jacobean playwright Thomas Middleton invented the concept of 'white people' on 29 October 1613, the date that his play The Triumphs of Truth was first performed. The phrase was first uttered by the character of an African king who looks out upon an English audience and declares: 'I see amazement set upon the faces/Of these white people, wond'rings and strange gazes.' As far as I, and others, have been able to tell, Middleton's play is the earliest printed example of a European author referring to fellow Europeans as 'white people'.

A year later, the English commoner John Rolfe of Jamestown in Virginia took as his bride an Algonquin princess named Matoaka, whom we call Pocahontas. The literary critic Christopher Hodgkins reports that King James I was 'at first perturbed when he learned of the marriage'. But this was not out of fear of miscegenation: James's reluctance, Hodgkins explained, was because 'Rolfe, a commoner, had without his sovereign's permission wed the daughter of a foreign prince.' King James was not worried about the pollution of Rolfe's line; he was worried about the pollution of Matoaka's.

Both examples might seem surprising to contemporary readers, but they serve to prove the historian Nell Irvin Painter's reminder in The History of White People (2010) that 'race is an idea, not a fact'. Middleton alone didn't invent the idea of whiteness, but the fact that anyone could definitely be the author of such a phrase, one that seems so obvious from a modern perspective, underscores Painter's point. By examining how and when racial concepts became hardened, we can see how historically conditional these concepts are. There's nothing essential about them. As the literature scholar Roxann Wheeler reminds us in The Complexion of Race (2000), there was 'an earlier moment in which biological racism... [was] not inevitable'. Since Europeans didn't always think of themselves as 'white', there is good reason to think that race is socially constructed, indeed arbitrary. If the idea of 'white people' (and thus every other 'race' as well) has a history – and a short one at that – then the concept itself is based less on any kind of biological reality than it is in the variable contingencies of social construction.

There are plenty of ways that one can categorise humanity, and using colour is merely a relatively recent one. In the past, criteria other than complexion were used, including religion, etiquette, even clothing. For example, American Indians were often compared with the ancient Britons by the colonisers, who were descendants of the Britons. The comparison was not so much physical as it was cultural, a distinction that allowed for a racial fluidity. Yet by the time Middleton was writing, the colour line was already beginning to harden, and our contemporary, if arbitrary, manner of categorising races began to emerge.

The scholar Kim Hall explains in Things of Darkness (1996) that whiteness 'truly exists only when posed next to blackness': so the concept of 'white people' emerged only after constructions of 'blackness'. As binary oppositions, 'whiteness' first needed 'blackness' to make any sense. The two words create each other. The scholar Virginia Mason Vaughan writes in Performing Blackness on English Stages, 1500-1800 (2005) that: 'Blackfaced characters in early modern dramas are often used ... to make whiteness visible.' 'Black' and 'white' have never referred to defined groups of people; they are abstract formulations, which still have had very real effects on actual people.

There is little verisimilitude in describing anyone with either term, which explains their malleability over the centuries. How arbitrary is it to categorise Sicilians and Swedes as being 'white', or the Igbo and Maasai as both 'black'? This kind of racial thinking developed as the direct result of the slave trade. Hall explains: 'Whiteness is not only constructed by but dependent on an involvement with Africans that is the inevitable product of England's ongoing colonial expansion.' As such, when early modern Europeans begin to think of themselves as 'white people' they are not claiming anything about being English, or Christian, but rather they are making comments about their self-perceived superiority, making it easier to justify the obviously immoral trade and ownership of humans.

Hall explains that the 'significance of blackness as a troping of race far exceeds the actual presence' of Africans within England at the time. Before Middleton's play, there were a host of imagined 'black' characters, such as in Ben Jonson's The Masque of Blackness ( )which featured Queen Anne performing in blackface, as well as Shakespeare's 'noble Moor' in Othello, staged a couple of years before Middleton's play. Understandings of race were malleable: in early modern writing, exoticised characters can be described as 'dusky', 'dun', 'dark', 'sable' or 'black.' Depictions of an exoticised Other weren't only of Africans, but also Italians, Spaniards, Arabs, Indians, and even the Irish. Middleton's play indicates the coalescing of another racial pole in contrast to blackness, and that's whiteness – but which groups belonged to which pole was often in flux.

Consider the Dark Lady of Shakespeare's sonnets. In sonnet 130, he says of his mysterious paramour that 'her breasts are dun'; in sonnet 12, he references her 'sable curls'; and in sonnet 127 he writes that 'black wires grow on her head'. As is commonly understood, and taught, Shakespeare subverted the tradition exemplified by poets such as Petrarch who conceptualised feminine beauty in terms of fairness. Part of this subversion lay in pronouncements such as the one that states that black is 'beauty's successive heir', a contention of Shakespeare's that can seem all the more progressive when our contemporary racial connotation of the word is considered. Thus, how much more radical is his argument in sonnet 132, that 'beauty herself is black/And all they foul that thy complexion lack.'

Shakespeare's racialised language connoted a range of possibilities as to how the Dark Lady's background could have been imagined, and the conjecture that she was based on women variously European or African indicates this racial flux in the period.

Or take Caliban, the native of the enchanted isle colonised by Prospero in The Tempest. Often sympathetically staged in modern productions as either an enslaved African or an American Indian, there are compelling reasons to think that many in a Jacobean audience would rather understand Caliban as being more akin to the first targets of English colonialism, the Irish. By this criterion, Caliban is part of the prehistory of 'how the Irish became white', as the historian Noel Ignatiev put it in 1995. None of this is to say that Caliban is actually any of these particular identities, nor that the Dark Lady should literally be identified as belonging to any specific group either, rather that both examples provide a window on the earliest period when our current racial categorisations began to take shape, while still being divergent enough from how our racialised system would ultimately develop.

Yet our particular criteria concerning how we think about race did develop, and it did so in service to colonialism and capitalism (and their handmaiden: slavery). Bolstered by a positivist language, the idea of race became so normalised that eventually the claim that anyone would have coined such an obvious phrase as 'white people' would begin to sound strange. But invented it was. With the re-emergence today of openly racist political rhetoric, often using disingenuously sophisticated terminology, it's crucial to remember what exactly it means to say that race isn't real, and why the claims of racists aren't just immoral, but also inaccurate. Middleton demonstrates how mercurial race actually is; there was a time not that long ago when white people weren't 'white', and black people weren't 'black'. His audience was just beginning to divide the world into white and not, and, unfortunately, we remain members of that audience.

Race might not be real, but racism very much is. Idols have a way of affecting our lives, even if the gods they represent are illusory. In contemplating Middleton's play, we can gesture towards a world where once again such a phrase as 'white people' won't make any sense. In realising that humans were not always categorised by complexion, we can imagine a future where we are no longer classified in such a way, and no longer divided as a result of it either.

[By: **Ed Simons,** staff writer at the literary site *The Millions* and an editor at *Berfrois*. His latest book is *Furnace of This World; or, 36 Observations about Goodness* (2019), and he is the author of *America and Other Fictions* (2018). He lives in Boston.

The article was originally published at https://aeon.co and has been republished under Creative Commons.]

Part four

Looking optimistically into the future

4

Looking optimistically into the future

I have now come to the end of my case. I want to repeat the main demand of this campaign.

It is calling for an end to the practice of calling humans black and white.

By way of a recap:

Objectively speaking there are no individual walking the surface of the earth endowed with black or white skin colours.

At medical school, I had the opportunity to study human skin in some detail. In the event, I realised that the architecture of human skin, irrespective of the colour of the individual, is identical.

Every human skin is endowed with melanocytes, which are responsible for the production of melanin, which endows the skin its brown to darkest brown hue. Melanin on its part shields the skin from the destructive effects of ultra-violet radiation

During my medical training, I also had the opportunity to witness children being born to mothers of different skin colours.

One fact that has left a lasting impression on my mind is that, whatever the background of the parents – European, African, Arab, Chinese – all of them arrive in the world with a light skin hue.

I want at this stage to introduce a personal element to the debate. When our daughter was born in a hospital in Hanover, for a while she became the star attraction on the postnatal ward. The majority of the staff, as well as the other new mothers on the ward, thought she would arrive in the world with a dark brown hue, just like her parents. On the contrary! The only clear difference between her outer appearance and those of the babies born to German parents was in regard to her dark black hair. Whereas many of the children born to German parents arrived with hardly any hair on their heads, she boasted black hair, indeed, abundant black hair!

As I mentioned in my main presentation, the concept of race is neither biological nor medically grounded.

The mechanism of childbirth follows an identical pattern irrespective of the background of the would-be mother; it is the same for any individual. Irrespective of their parents, babies usually spend 40 weeks in their mother's womb.

I also want to draw the attention of the jury to the issue of blood groups – they are randomly distributed among all types of humans, whether they call Africa or America or Asia or Europe, their home.

The heart of every human being is located in the left upper area of the chest, irrespective of whether an individual is "black" or "white". Of course there are very rare instances when the heart is malpositioned somewhere else in the body – the right side of the chest, in the stomach, within the diaphragm etc. That is, however, a rare medical anomaly and is not dependent on "race".

Paracetamol (Acetaminophen) is able to reduce the temperature of everyone with a fever, irrespective of whether the individual's skin colour is the chocolate brown of the author of these lines or the pale colour of an Eskimo. I could go on citing examples until every single member of the jury falls asleep – out of sheer boredom!

As I mentioned in my main presentation, the arbitrary classification of humans into black and white dates back about 400 years.

I find it extraordinary how much the practice of designating humans as "black" and "white" has been so narrowed, so restricted to the African population south of the Sahara on the one side and the European on the other.

I studied medicine in Germany. I practised in that country for more than a decade before moving to the UK. As a medical student, and later as a doctor, I have come into contact with fellow students and colleagues as well as patients from places like India, Sri Lanka, Iran, Vietnam, Bangladesh etc., individuals whose skin hue is darker than, for example, an Ibgo of Nigeria – yet the Igbo is called black whereas an individual from India is an Indian or Asian! Conversely, people from China or Japan, individuals whose skin colour might be fairer than a south European, are called Chinese or Japanese whereas a person from southern Europe is classified as being white.

Over time we seem to have become familiar with the concept, giving rice to terms like "black beauty", "black panther", "white supremacy", "white", "black", "black lives matters" etc.

The fact that everyone seems to have come to terms with the present classification, in my view, does not prevent us from dealing with the fundamental issue of misrepresentation of the facts at the root of the classification.

These days the talk is of institutional racism. In my view, the concept of black and white is at the very root of institutional racism. It is a kind of apartheid in the use of words. How else should I describe it, when everyone speaks of "Black Monday" when the stock exchange collapses, but on the other hand when cases are won, people tend to wear the white flags and hoist white banners.

Whereas for the short term we could perhaps live with a terminology forced upon us by others, in my opinion that should not be allowed to persist in perpetuity.

Whereas at the moment campaign groups such as Black Lives Matter are doing what it takes to put the issue of discrimination against people of African descent into the limelight, five to ten years from now the campaign may no longer be in the news. On the other hand, if steps are not taken to end at least the official use of the term "black" without delay, it will continue into perpetuity, with all the negative connotations associated with it.

Universally, the words "black" and "white" are associated with evil and good respectively. The power of association is enormous. The fact that black is bad and white is good leads others to associate so-called "black" people with evil and so-called "white" people with good. Such a practice leads among other things to "institutional racism". That is one of the reasons I am calling for an end to the practice.

I hold the view that it is against the Divine plan to categorise humans as black, since evidentially no one was created black or white.

Even those who do not believe in God – even those who call themselves atheist or humanist or agnostic or whatever – will bear me out that it is against the principle of fairness to classify humans as black and white, since no one of us is endowed with such types of skin colour.

Someone will ask me – if you are requesting the relinquishing of those two designations, what should be the alternatives.

Personally, I would call for the doing away of the practice of categorising human beings entirely. Everyone should just be called a human being, a resident of planet earth.

Since such a classification will be considered utopian by the vast majority of the world's population, I would suggest, as an alternative, that people are referred to by their country of birth – British, German, Ghanaian, Russian etc.

Alternatively, we could modify the current system to meet the demands of the campaign by referring to people of African descent as Africans and those of European descent as Europeans. Under this system, children born to African-European couples would receive the designation: African-European.

In the event that society still insists on the use of colours to describe the two population groups at the heart of this campaign, we could go for chocolate brown for Africans and peach or orange coloured for their European counterparts.

I have no illusions that such a step alone will do away with the prejudices that humans harbour in their minds, overnight change attitudes and behaviour cultivated over generations.

This fact, ladies and gentlemen of the jury, was poignantly brought home to me only a couple of days ago. On 2 July 2020, just as I was seated in front of my laptop and was in the process of preparing this closing statement, I decided to quickly check the daily headlines online. It was then that I encountered a BBC online news report that left me flabbergasted beyond measure. I was indeed so shocked that for a while I could not believe my eyes regarding what I was reading.

In the news report, a well-known British TV historian was quoted as saying the following in an online interview the previous day: "Slavery was not genocide. Otherwise there wouldn't be so many damn blacks in Africa or Britain, would there?"

It is generally held that education refines thinking and thoughts. Higher education does not turn humans into angels, but it is supposed to make them develop the habit of weighing their words carefully, thinking carefully about the impact their words might have on others, before uttering them.

So I did not expect an academic, an individual who holds a doctorate degree in his field of endeavour, to make such a demeaning statement, an assertion that goes below the belt, an utterance that is cruel, inhumane, disgraceful, reprehensible ...

you can go on listing all the English words in use for such a blatant display of disrespect and insensitivity to others.

I am from Ghana, the former Gold Coast. My hometown is about 50 miles from the Atlantic Ocean. The learned historian might be aware of the fact that the stretch of the coastline in question used to be called the Slave Coast. Dotted on the so-called Slave Coast are several castles that served as the basis for the transatlantic slave trade.

I want to highlight one of them, namely the Cape Coast Castle. It ended up as one of the main slave trade fortresses of the then Gold Coast. A large dungeon was specially constructed beneath the building at the peak of the trade in humans to serve as a "warehouse" for the slaves as they awaited the arrival of the ships to transport them to the faraway lands of the Americas and the Caribbean islands. The dungeon could aptly be described as a compartment of misery, terror and death. Indeed not an insignificant number of the slaves perished in the hot, congested and poorly ventilated compartment long before they could set out on the perilous journey across the Atlantic to their final destinations.

When they were finally marched against their wills through "the door of no return", located on the seaboard side of the fortress, their doom were sealed. Emerging from the "door of no return" the slaves were lowered into boats, and then loaded like cargo onto big slave ships further out at sea – never to see their beloved family members and their homeland again.

There are no records to this effect, but I can well imagine that if not several then at least a few of my direct ancestors – great, great, great, uncles, aunts, cousins and nieces, from the lines of both of my parents suffered the same fate as the millions who passed through the "gates of no return" of the several slave castles dotted along the Ghanaian coast.... Sorry, members of the jury, I am becoming quite emotional... especially in view of what I am about to reveal. On not a few occasions I have come across individuals of African descent, who bear such a close resemblance to some members of both my nuclear and extended family, who now call places like Jamaica, Brazil, the US etc. their home! In such moments, I become nervous and battle with my tears at the thought that they could well be my relations!

Mr "Doctor of History", my ancestors might well have been considered primitive by your posh ancestors – and forgive me if none of your ancestors was directly involved in the inhumane trade! But people from your "white," race surely were. Indeed my ancestors might have been considered primitive by your ancestors, but they were living peacefully in their God-given land! They might have been dying early from malaria and other diseases – and so what? As someone put it "we all face the death penalty". For some, the sentence may be executed a few hours after their arrival on earth, even before they have had any time to settle. Some manage to make it past a century – the fact is that at the end of the day we all face the inevitable.

You might also regard the "damn blacks" as primitive and barbarian, who deserved to be forced, at the point of the gun, from their homes and sold into far away land against their will. Who is the barbarian in this respect, the inhumane perpetrator of the awful deeds or the innocent, unarmed victims –children as well as defenceless women, some of whom were pregnant with children?

No one is demanding from the "Honourable Doctor" that he undoes the evils of the past. No one is accusing him of direct involvement in the inhumane trade that depleted Africa of well over ten million of her children. But to utter such despicable words, to maintain such a mindset in the twenty-first century – that is really shocking!

I am not trying to falsely accuse you of anything, but your words lead me to think that if you had happened to encounter the scene where poor Mr George Floyd's neck was being compressed by the knee of the police officer to the point of asphyxiation, you would not have intervened. I am just conjecturing that you probably might have cheered the perpetrator on!

Ladies and gentlemen of the jury, as the above example illustrates, stopping the use of the reference to black and white will not automatically end the disdain and disrespect others harbour for people of African descent.

Ladies and gentlemen, you are certainly familiar with the half-empty and half-full approach to a bottle filled to the middle with water. Personally, I have an optimistic approach to life, so I want to take the half-full perspective on the matter.

It is my view that relinquishing the use of the designation, ceasing from the practice of officially categorising individuals as "black" and "white", will be a first step in the right direction.

I am looking into the future, say 50 or 100 years from now – into a world where, at least, the official use of the terms "black" and "white" to categorise human beings would be a thing of the past.

I am looking into the future, looking at a time when children born into the world will not have to be told that black people are associated with evil and that white people are associated with good.

I am thinking of those who will be born into a world where their opinions about people of African descent would not be marred from the onset by the fact they are called black – they will not automatically be tempted or inclined to think them evil by virtue of associating the colour black with evil.

Ladies and gentlemen of the world jury, the idea of "blacks" who are inferior and evil, sold into slavery to "white" slave masters, has remained a burden on a section of God's children.

So long as humans are designated black, which they are not, and whites, which they are not, this discrimination will be perpetuated into eternity.

As the saying goes, it is never too late to begin something. The terminologies are barely 400 years old. If we take the bold initiative today towards getting rid of the terminologies, 400 years from now future generations will look back and reminisce on the tensions it caused in the past and rejoice over the positive contribution it has made towards social cohesion and understanding among people of different backgrounds.

So in conclusion, ladies and gentlemen of the jury, I am leaving you to make a decision, based on the testimony and information provided.

Now you have heard all the evidence and the arguments, it is your duty to follow your conscience and arrive at a judgement, based on the facts of the case.

Without doubt some of you may have preconceived ideas and opinions on the matter. The case before you, however, is not about opinions. Instead it is about the facts and your sense of fairness.

Regardless of any opinion you may have or your preconceived opinions, it would be a violation of your conscience to discard the evidence and decide based on your preformed opinions. Indeed I implore you not to be swayed by bias or favour. Instead you should base your verdict upon the evidence presented.

I stated in my presentation the fact that the colour black so far has not had any lobby in world affairs. I pray you not to be biased against the colour black because others consider it normal so to do. I implore you to refrain from any form of bias or prejudice towards the colour black.

Your duty instead is to carefully and impartially consider all the evidence in the case and reach a just verdict regardless of the consequences.

I also urge you to keep the photo report and the articles submitted in support of the case in your mind as you deliberate on your decision in the matter.

You are the sole judges of the credibility or "believability" of the evidence so presented to you. In weighing the testimony so as to form an opinion, you should allow candour, fairness and intelligence be your best advisers.

As a result of the foregoing, the campaign is appealing to the world jury to side with it and to support our cause.

Finally, I am aware that not everyone involved believes in the Bible. Still, I want to quote from the Holy Book to conclude my case.

"So God created humankind in his image, in the image of God he created them; male and female He created them." (Genesis 1:27 (NRSV))

God did not create black and white. Instead, He created humankind in His image. Why should we then categorise humans into black and white, into two so-called "distinct races" when indeed there is one, and only one, human race.

Distinguished ladies and gentlemen of the jury, I hereby rest my case!

www.ingramcontent.com/pod-product-compliance
Lightning Source LLC
Chambersburg PA
CBHW050529280326
41933CB00011B/1521